Bristol

Historic and Flourishing

CONTENTS

New development in traditional surroundings - housing at Merchants Landing and the Lloyds Bank Canon's Marsh site

Everyone agrees – Bristol is the most pleasant large city in England. It has grown spaciously over several hills around the River Avon, leaving generous open areas within its boundaries, and yet nowhere in the city seems too far from the country. Indeed, from the heart of the city it is possible to glimpse the green of Dundry Hill or Ashton Park to the south or west, and the West Country speech of the Bristolian seems to bring in a breath of country air.

This is a gateway city, always on a frontier. Across the Severn Estuary, Wales is visible on a clear day, and the nearby Severn Bridge and Severn Tunnel provide the main road and rail links to South Wales. Bristol also stands beside the junction of the M4 and the M5, and many holidaymakers pass by on their way to Devon and Cornwall, feeling as they reach Bristol that they have just arrived in the West Country.

The city has traditionally stood on the boundary between Somerset and Gloucestershire; north of the River Avon, Bristol was in Gloucestershire, to the south it was in Somerset. Although the city's charter of 1373 gave it the status of city and county, there were anomalies, and to this day it remains possible to watch Gloucestershire play county cricket in Bristol. The new county of Avon at last recognises the importance of Bristol, making it the centre of a county which also includes Bath. And in its history, the port of Bristol was a gateway to an even wider world – the colonies of North America.

The pleasantness of modern Bristol is a tribute to the city's development during the past thousand years. For much of this time it has been England's most successful city outside London, and one of her main seaports. It was trade with Europe and America which encouraged those traditional Bristol industries – tobacco, chocolate and wine – and the wealth generated by this commercial activity paid for much new building in the city. Bristol has always meant commerce, and throughout its history, the great benefactors of the city have been merchants and businessmen like Edward Colston, the Wills family, and John James.

Bristol is an enterprising and a pioneering city. From this port John Cabot set sail on a voyage which was to lead to his discovery of the mainland of America; Brunel's SS *Great Britain* – the world's first iron-hulled propeller-driven vessel, and the largest ship then built – was launched here; and more recently, Concorde was built here.

This pioneering spirit perhaps explains the unruly, free-ranging appearance of Bristol. The present-day city lacks a coherent centre, and though there is an abundance of historic buildings, there are few monumental public buildings. Bristol has never been a capital city; it never had an ancient university; only for the briefest periods has it been at the centre of fashion. Yet it is for all these reasons that Bristol has, in fact, remained successful – enterprise, hard work and adaptability have always been its vital qualities. 'Virtute et Industria' proclaims the city's motto: virtue and hard work.

In Bristol, a working as well as a historic city, the old and the new nestle together throughout, and the tourist in a hurry who seeks a quick impression could be disappointed. But add the

sum of all the different parts, and Bristol looks incomparable. Take St Mary Redcliffe – there is no finer parish church in England; add to this the medieval towers of St Stephen's and the Temple Church, and the Norman remains of St Augustine's Abbey (now the cathedral). Consider those timber-framed houses which survive, and take note of the great number of Georgian houses and churches, for the eighteenth century was Bristol's golden age. Don't forget Clifton Suspension Bridge, perhaps the strongest single image of the city, or the Wills Memorial Building which has become a familiar part of the Bristol skyline since 1925. Bristol can also be proud of the later twentieth century – the docks have been re-developed for leisure use, warehouses have been restored and converted, and new buildings have been fitted into the pattern of a historic city.

Leisure activities are important here, and the leisure industry is big business. Where once ocean-going vessels were constructed, small workshops now repair leisure craft; where busy commercial traffic once passed, sailboards and dinghies now enjoy the challenge of the water. Where recently there was dereliction, now there is new housing and access to the water's edge. Look into the sky on a warm day in August and you will probably see a hot-air balloon, perhaps drifting across the city from the Balloon Fiesta in Ashton Park. Bristolians have always been adventurers, and they continue to demand new excitement and new challenges.

This is not the only pattern to have emerged from the last twenty years in Bristol. The pleasant atmosphere and the good communications with London, by motorway and high-speed train, have encouraged companies to relocate here. Above all, Bristol has become one of the main centres for banking and insurance outside London, and new office buildings have been filling in the gaps in previous developments. In some of its buildings, especially around Bond Street from the Spectrum Building to Castlemead House, Bristol presents a modern commercial face. In others, such as Broad Quay House and the Bristol & West extension, new buildings are traditional in appearance, taking their cue from the remaining warehouse buildings around the docks.

Many visitors will share the same thoughts: with so much to see, and so far to travel between sights, what to choose and where to go? In order to simplify this confusion, we are suggesting the three areas of the city that should not be missed. First the old city, based around Corn Street, but spreading out to include St Mary Redcliffe and the cathedral and Park Street area. Second, the city docks, situated close to the old city, but conveniently thought of as a different area as it could involve a boat trip or a quayside walk, and could include a visit to the SS *Great Britain*. Finally there is Clifton, a little further from the city centre, where the suspension bridge over the Avon Gorge, the Downs, the zoo and the crescents and terraces all have their special appeal.

Enjoy a city which has so much to offer, a historic city with a flourishing commercial life. Explore its streets and waterways and enjoy its lively atmosphere. Visit its beautiful neighbour, incomparable Georgian Bath; visit Cheddar Gorge and Wells Cathedral. But return to Bristol.

Bristol Cathedral – originally St Augustine's Abbey – was raised to its present status in 1542

3

Trade and Commerce

Bristol developed from Saxon 'Brigstow', the place by the bridge, and the river with its access to the sea was for centuries Bristol's source of wealth. In the Middle Ages, Bristol merchants traded as far afield as Portugal and Iceland, exchanging woollen cloth for such commodities as wine and fish. By this time the city's crest – a ship sailing out from a castle – had become established as Bristol's trademark.

Bristol merchants became so powerful, and the city had become so useful in wartime for its ships, that in 1373 King Edward III granted Bristol a charter which not only gave the city certain liberties, but declared it a county in its own right. Until then, most of Bristol north of the river had been in Gloucestershire, while the growing suburbs to the south, including the church of St Mary Redcliffe, had been in Somerset. At the same time the Mayor was given the right to have a sword of state carried in front of him, and this ceremonial sword survives, the oldest civic sword in England.

Maritime trade was always an adventure – money was ventured and lives were risked, but the rewards could be fantastic. This sense of speculation and adventure meant that stories of new lands and great

Above: *The 'nails' on Corn Street were used for commercial transactions, hence 'to pay on the nail'; behind, Lloyds Bank is lavishly Venetian in style*

Below: *The statue of Neptune presides over St Augustine's Reach; to each side there are quayside walks with* (opposite) *new offices at Broad Quay House*

riches circulated among the Bristol merchants. One such tale concerned the 'Isle of Brazil', rumoured to be to the west of Ireland. In 1480 a Bristol ship set sail in search of this land – twelve years before the famous voyage of Christopher Columbus. After nine weeks sailing in the Atlantic Ocean, the ship was driven back to Ireland, with no new discoveries, but with the spirit of adventure undaunted.

This was to be only the beginning of Bristol's connection with the Americas. In 1497 a Venetian who had settled in Bristol, John Cabot, gained the confidence of his fellow merchants and set sail westward on a voyage of discovery. His ship was the *Matthew,* and the crew of eighteen included his son, Sebastian, who had been born in Bristol. Five years earlier, Columbus had sailed from Spain on a southerly route, eventually landing in the West Indies. Cabot chose the northerly passage remembered in Norse mythology, and after fifty-two days at sea sighted a 'new found land'. In this way, a Bristol voyage claims first discovery of the mainland of America.

Many more voyages were made by Sebastian Cabot and others, and Bristol became the main place of departure for those emigrating to America in the seventeenth century. It is not too fanciful to imagine, in

Left: *The Granary on Welsh Back – Victorian warehouse in 'Bristol Byzantine' style*

Below: *A mock-up of Concorde can be explored in Bristol's Industrial Museum*

THE POWER TO FLY

the burred 'r' of the American accent, a reflection of the West Country English spoken in Bristol.

Trade with North America gave the city its greatest period of wealth. By 1700 Bristol had become the largest city in England outside London, and in the eighteenth century Bristol's ships brought tobacco, rum and sugar to the city, fostering the cigarette and chocolate industries which still survive. Part of this trade involved the heartless transportation of African slaves to America; in 1725 alone, Bristol ships carried 16,950 slaves to the plantations. In fairness, the Quakers and Methodists, both strong in Bristol, did oppose this cruel trade, and slavery was eventually abolished in the British colonies sooner than elsewhere.

This new wealth contributed to much new building in the city. Suburbs with Georgian squares and terraces were developed at Kingsdown, St Paul's, Hotwells and Clifton, and large houses for wealthy merchants appeared at Kings Weston, Henbury and Redland as well as Clifton. But the commercial building which best reflects this age of improvement is the Exchange on Corn Street, designed by John Wood of Bath. Its swaggering classical façade makes a strong statement about the new wealth and civic pride of Bristol's merchants.

The nineteenth century was a time of relative decline, with Liverpool and Glasgow overtaking Bristol's west-coast maritime activity. Yet this relatively slow growth can now be seen as a good thing – because Bristol has never depended on just one industry, the problems of too rapid growth or recession have been less acute there. The city docks had for so long been in decline that the eventual closing to commercial traffic did not leave too ugly a scar on the city; indeed, the regeneration of the docks for leisure activities has been Bristol's great triumph. With a modern container port and much of Bristol's heavier industry at Avonmouth, this has left the city centre open for clean-air commerce – banking and insurance.

Bristol's connection with the wine trade continues with Harveys, who sell their 'Bristol Cream' throughout the world; Wills still manufacture cigarettes, and Fry's still make chocolate (though now owned by Cadbury-Schweppes). But perhaps the most famous product of a Bristol factory has been Concorde, the Anglo-French supersonic passenger aeroplane. At the time when that other Bristol-made pioneer, the SS *Great Britain,* was being brought back to the city docks, Concorde was soaring over the Bristol skies on its test flights. Neither one, ship nor jet, may have been an immediate commercial success, but both have the capacity to make people stop and stare, and both will surely long be remembered.

Top right: *The Merchant Venturers Almshouses on King Street are overshadowed by more recent developments*

Centre right: *The Spectrum Building on Bond Street – a reflection of things to come?*

Bottom right: *Flags and flowerbeds adorn the Centre, the hub of modern commercial Bristol*

9

Brunel's Bristol

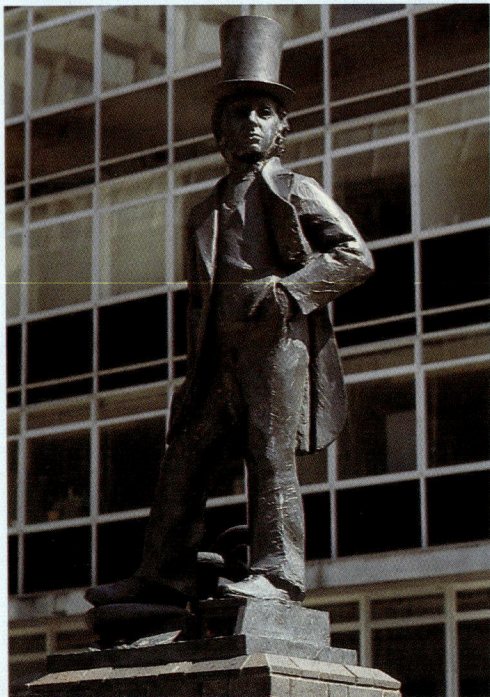

The unique genius of Isambard Kingdom Brunel can be clearly appreciated in Bristol. One of his first independent designs was for a suspension bridge to span the Avon Gorge at Clifton – this was, however, rejected on the advice of Thomas Telford. Two years later, in 1831, Brunel's modified design was accepted as winner in a competition, beating one of Telford's own designs. Work began on the bridge in 1836, but because of cash shortages it was not completed until 1864, five years after Brunel's death. More than a hundred years later the bridge is still in everyday use, carrying commuters and shoppers from satellite villages in what was once Somerset, taking Bristolians out to the fresh air of Ashton Court or Leigh Woods, or ferrying reluctant schoolboys across for an afternoon of sport at the playing fields beyond.

In 1833, Brunel was appointed chief engineer to the Great Western Railway. He planned the line from London to Bristol, built its famous stone bridges over the Thames, and engineered the tunnel at Box, beyond Bath. Not satisfied with civil engineering, he also designed two notable buildings connected with the railway in Bristol, one being Temple Meads Station. This was the original station, built in 1841, which still survives, facing busy Temple Gate and to the left of the present station buildings. The front is built in castellated Tudor style; the huge engine shed behind is more functional, yet decorated with false hammerbeams and Tudor arches. Together, these form the earliest surviving railway terminus buildings in the world.

Brunel's other Bristol building is a vestige of an even greater vision than the Great Western Railway alone. Many visitors to Bristol are confused by the position of Temple Meads Station away from the city centre. Brunel's plan was for the Great Western Railway terminus to be north of the cathedral close, nearer to the city, and much nearer to the docks. This plan was overruled, but not before part of it had been executed – a Royal Western Hotel, which was to have housed passengers arriving from London by train, before they embarked on the voyage to New York by steamship. Bristol was to have been the pivotal point in the journey; the transport was to be provided by Brunel's Great Western Railway and his *Great Western* steamship.

As it happened, this vision never came to pass. Although as engineer to the Bristol docks Brunel made improvements to the new floating harbour which kept Bristol competitive for a few more decades, bigger ships could only mean bigger docks. His

Top left: Isambard Kingdom Brunel, the great engineer, is commemorated by this recent Bristol statue

Centre left: The train shed of Brunel's original Great Western Railway terminus

Bottom left: The Royal Western Hotel, now Brunel House, was intended for passengers on his railways and steamships

Bristol-built *Great Western* of 1837 was the largest ship then built, and the first paddle steamer used in a regular service between Britain and America (the voyage took fifteen days) – and Brunel planned still larger vessels.

The *Great Britain* was the world's first iron-hulled propeller-driven steamship. Launched in Bristol in 1843, she measured 722 feet in length, weighed 1,936 tons, and could accommodate 760 passengers. She made several voyages to America, and was then used for twenty-one years to take emigrants to Australia. Later she was converted to a sailing ship, but ran aground in the Falkland Islands where she was afterwards used as a coal hulk. The story has a happy ending, however. In 1970 she was brought back to Bristol; the writer remembers the sight of her rusty hull being edged slowly along the river beneath the suspension bridge, which Brunel never lived to see completed. Now, in the very dry dock where she was built, the painstaking work of restoration continues, a tribute to a moment in Bristol's history, and to the achievements of Isambard Kingdom Brunel.

The SS Great Britain *is being restored in the dry dock where she was first built*

The Old City

Bristol has grown so fast from the days when it was a settlement between the rivers Avon and Frome, that the modern city could be thought to lack cohesion. The visitor arriving for the first time at Temple Meads station would have difficulty finding the old city, let alone Clifton or Broadmead shopping centre.

The city's waterways are complicated; neither Bristol's magnificent parish church – St Mary Redcliffe – nor its cathedral were built within the walls of the medieval city; and to add to the confusion, post-war planners have altered parts of the old city left alone by the bombs of November 1940. Yet there is much in the heart of old Bristol to reward a visit.

The point where High Street, Corn Street, Broad Street and Wine Street meet is the very heart of the old city and the traditional site of Bristol's medieval market cross. The paved section of Corn Street offers the incomparable sight of John Wood's classical Exchange fronted by the four brass 'nails' upon which merchants made their transactions (hence the expression 'to pay on the nail'). To the side are an eighteenth-century coffee house and the cupola tower of All Saints Church; opposite is the lavish Venetian-style Lloyds Bank, and over the road are the quarter-jacks on Christchurch, which strike each quarter of an hour. The poet Southey, as a boy, used to stop here to watch them. Alleyways to either side of the Exchange lead into the eighteenth-century covered market.

High Street leads to Bristol Bridge, from where that part of the old city devastated in the Blitz can clearly be seen. The area is now a grassy park, with the gutted remains of St Peter's Church a focal point. Beyond this is the site of Bristol Castle, once so important, and now only commemorated in the name, Castle Park. Across the river is a commercial area, worth visiting for two reasons. One is the church of St Mary Redcliffe, a pleasure many visitors expect; the other is the entirely unexpected sight of the leaning tower of the Temple Church, glimpsed along Church Lane. The tower, which leans five feet out of true, was clearly already a problem in the Middle Ages because its uppermost section attempts to correct the earlier lean.

Broad Street – one of the narrower streets in the old city – leads towards St John's Church, whose tower and spire are built over the last surviving medieval gateway. Notice on the right the extraordinary Art Nouveau ceramic-tiled front of Edward Everard's Printing House with its painted figures celebrating Gutenberg, the inventor of printing, and William Morris, who championed the revival of traditional crafts. Beyond St John's Gate, across busy Lewins Mead, can be found the concealed pleasures of Christmas Steps, a narrow street of craft and collectors' shops which, it is recorded, was paved in 1669. At the foot of the steps are the doorway of a medieval

St Peter's Church, and St Mary-le-Port behind, were casualties of the Blitz in 1940

hospital and a group of restored timber-framed buildings. Further on, beyond the top of Christmas Steps, St Michael's Hill is a street of seventeenth-century town houses which leads steeply away from the centre, offering good views back towards the towers and spires of the city.

Corn Street leads from the heart of the medieval town towards what is now known as the Centre – the road system with its flowerbeds which conceals the course of the River Frome. Until the last century, ships would moor here, right beside the elongated Perpendicular tower of St Stephen's. Broad Quay and Narrow Quay, facing each other across St Augustine's Reach, are the best place to begin an exploration of the city docks, and round to the right, College Green is enclosed by the cathedral, the Council House and Park Street, which climbs up to the impressive Wills Memorial Building of Bristol University.

To the south side of the medieval city, in an area developed in the seventeenth-century, stand Bristol's grandest square and most picturesque street. Queen

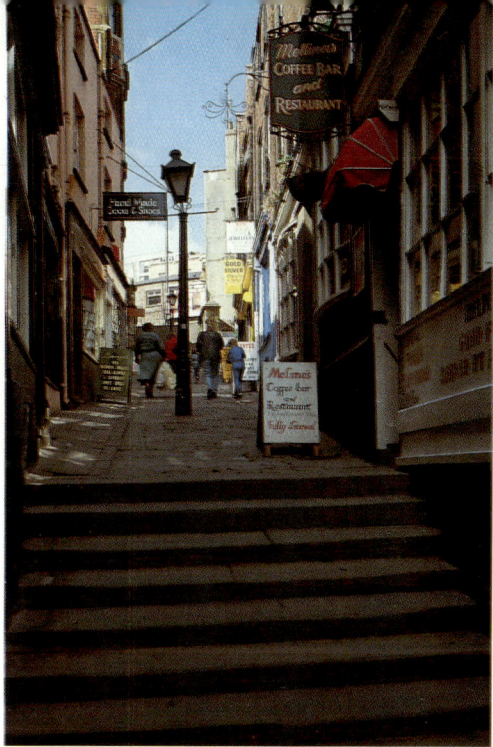

Left: *St Nicholas Church, by Bristol Bridge, is now a branch of the City Museum*

Below: *Inside the Exchange on Corn Street*

Above: *Christmas Steps is a picturesque narrow street which climbs steeply away from the city centre*

Square is one of the earliest – and largest – squares in England, and although the Reform Law riots of 1831 left the Mansion House and Customs House looted, and two sides of the square in flames, it is still an impressive sight. In the centre of the square, on a traffic island, is Rysbrack's statue of King William III on horseback in heroic Roman guise. King Street, with its cobbles and historic buildings, is the place where Bristol's seafaring past can be felt most strongly. The Merchant Venturers' Almshouses, intended for retired seamen, form two sides of the original quadrangle; the Old Library, now a restaurant, is where Coleridge and Southey used to read; the Theatre Royal, which opened in 1766, is a famous provincial theatre; the Naval Volunteer is reminiscent of Bristol's maritime past and the Llandoger Trow is Bristol's most spectacular timber-framed building.

Left: *Cobbled King Street is Bristol's showpiece with its ancient buildings and its modern entertainments*

Below: *William III strikes a regal pose over Queen Square in Rysbrack's famous sculpture*

Churches

Queen Elizabeth I described St Mary Redcliffe as the 'fairest, goodliest and most famous parish church in England'. With its tall spire, transepts, flying buttresses and soaring Perpendicular windows it is indeed a grand sight, and unlike so many town churches, its interior does not disappoint. Sitting in the nave, you are conscious of the piers rising without interruption to the gold-embossed vault, giving a sense of loftiness unmatched even by any English cathedral.

Why is it that Bristol should have a parish church with cathedral-like proportions? How is it that this grandest of city churches should have been built outside the city, across the river in Somerset? The answer to these questions lies in the wealth of the merchants of Redcliffe who gave money to the glory of God, and to the magnificence of their church which could rival anything across the river. Most famous of all these merchant benefactors was William Canynges, five times Mayor, twice Member of Parliament for Bristol, and the owner of a larger fleet than any other Bristol merchant of the fifteenth century. After the death of his wife, Canynges renounced the world of commerce, and entered the church as a priest; green rushes are scattered on the floor of the church each Whitsun in a ceremony of commemoration of this event. The tombs of William Canynges and his wife can be found in the church.

Top left: *The Norman chapter-house at the cathedral*

Centre left: *Stained glass in the Catholic Cathedral*

Bottom left: *The imposing modern exterior of the Catholic Cathedral*

Below: *Quarterjacks above the doorway at Christchurch, Broad Street*

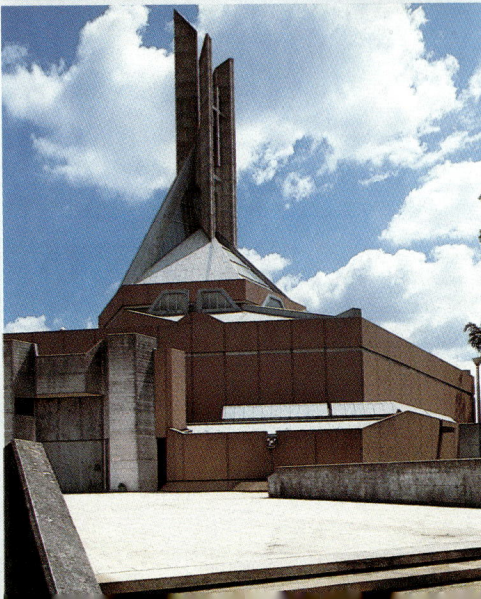

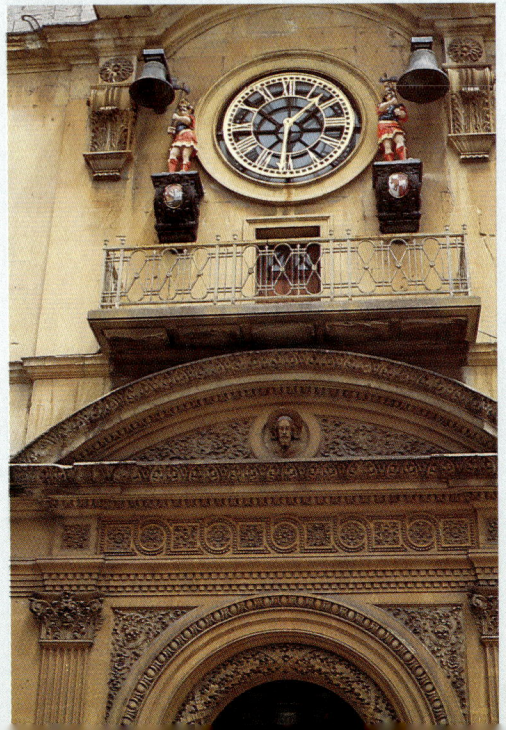

Bristol Cathedral was originally the Abbey of St Augustine, being granted cathedral status by Henry VIII after the Dissolution of the Monasteries. Its Norman chapter-house is lavishly decorated with blank arches and zigzag ornament, creating an impressively abstract design. The eastern arm of the church was built in the early fourteenth century, and is unusual in that the aisles rise as high as the chancel, and are supported with internal flying buttresses. Pevsner, the architectural historian, describes this design as 'from the point of view of spatial imagination . . . superior to anything else built in England and indeed in Europe at the same time'. The church was never completed during the Middle Ages; the nave and west towers are Victorian additions.

Bristol is closely associated with the history of Nonconformism. In 1739 John Wesley came to Bristol to preach, and his New Room in Broadmead became the world's first Methodist chapel. Inside, the double-decker pulpit from which he preached is illuminated by a central octagonal dome which rises through the living accommodation above, affording glimpses down into the chapel. Nearby, the Quakers held their first meetings in the old Dominican Friary, hence the improbable name Quakers' Friars. It was here that William Penn, founder of Pennsylvania, was married. Today these buildings house a registry office and a permanent planning exhibition.

The most impressive modern church in Bristol is the Roman Catholic Cathedral in Clifton, which was consecrated in 1973. From the outside, the building looks stark, surmounted with its plain concrete spire. Inside the simply and sparsely decorated building, the atmosphere is surprisingly light and warm.

St Mary Redcliffe – the finest parish church in England
Inset: *St Stephen's Church tower*

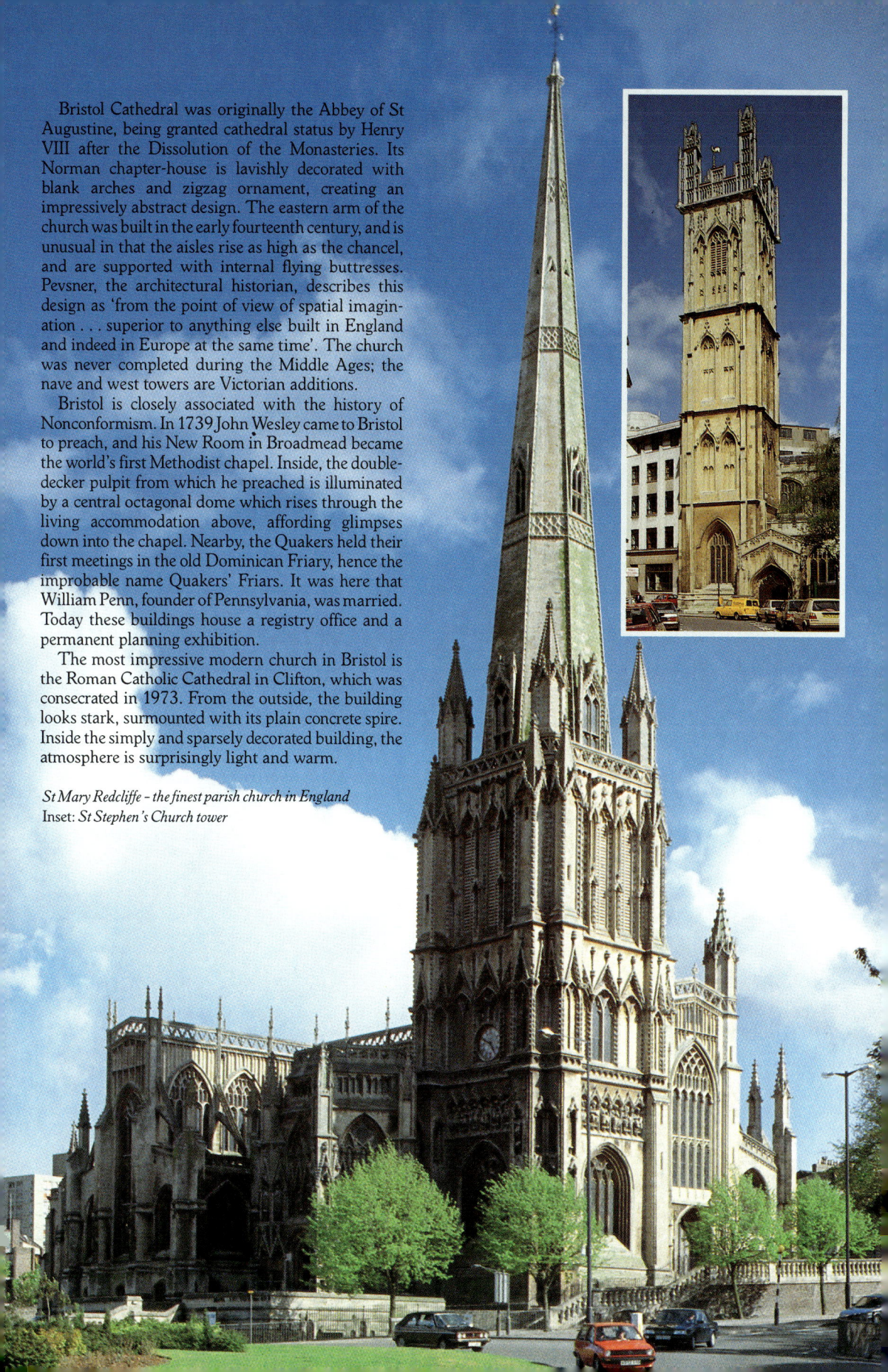

Nowhere in central Bristol is far from the river, and the presence of seagulls is a reminder of the closeness of the sea. The city's waterways are confusing to the visitor, however, consisting of two rivers – the Avon and the Frome – as well as the New Cut, engineered when the Avon became the floating harbour.

The wharves of medieval Bristol were along Welsh Back towards Bristol Bridge and along the River Frome by the Centre. Improvements started as early as the thirteenth century when the citizens dug a new channel for the Frome, redirecting it along St Augustine's Reach. For another 500 years the docks remained tidal, which meant that with the ebb of each tide, a ship could settle awkwardly in the mud, and risk breaking its back.

In response to this problem, a scheme to retain a constant water level in the Avon, allowing ships to float at all times – a floating harbour – was begun in 1804. The tidal river was diverted along a new channel, the New Cut, which was connected to the floating harbour by a system of locks. Those at Cumberland Basin form the main entrance to the harbour.

One problem of the floating harbour was the very lack of a tide to remove sewage and to prevent silting; another was the high dues charged to pay for these improvements. Brunel was appointed engineer to the Bristol docks, and he was able to solve the problem of silting. However, the tidal River Avon and the floating harbour ultimately became impractical for larger vessels.

The docks finally closed to commercial traffic in the early 1970s, and a determined effort was made to find new uses for the area. These schemes have now come to fruition, and few other places can offer marinas, a caravan park and even windsurfing in the heart of a large city.

The best starting point for an exploration of the docks is the statue of Neptune, by the Centre. On Broad Quay former warehouse buildings are now used as an arts and media centre – the Watershed. Opening onto the quayside are speciality shops which do a good trade at weekends and on public holidays. Beyond is the Bristol Exhibition Centre, home to the annual World Wine Fair among other events.

Narrow Quay offers a cobbled walk past moored boats towards the Arnolfini, a now famous arts centre in a former tea warehouse. Across the bridge on Princes Wharf is the Bristol Industrial Museum, with its mock-up of Concorde and its exhibition of Bristol's maritime history. From here there is also one of the

Top left: John Cabot looks west, in a recent sculpture outside the Arnolfini

Bottom left: The Cabot Tower commemorates the discovery of the mainland of America in 1497

Right: Statue of Edward Colston, Bristol merchant and benefactor

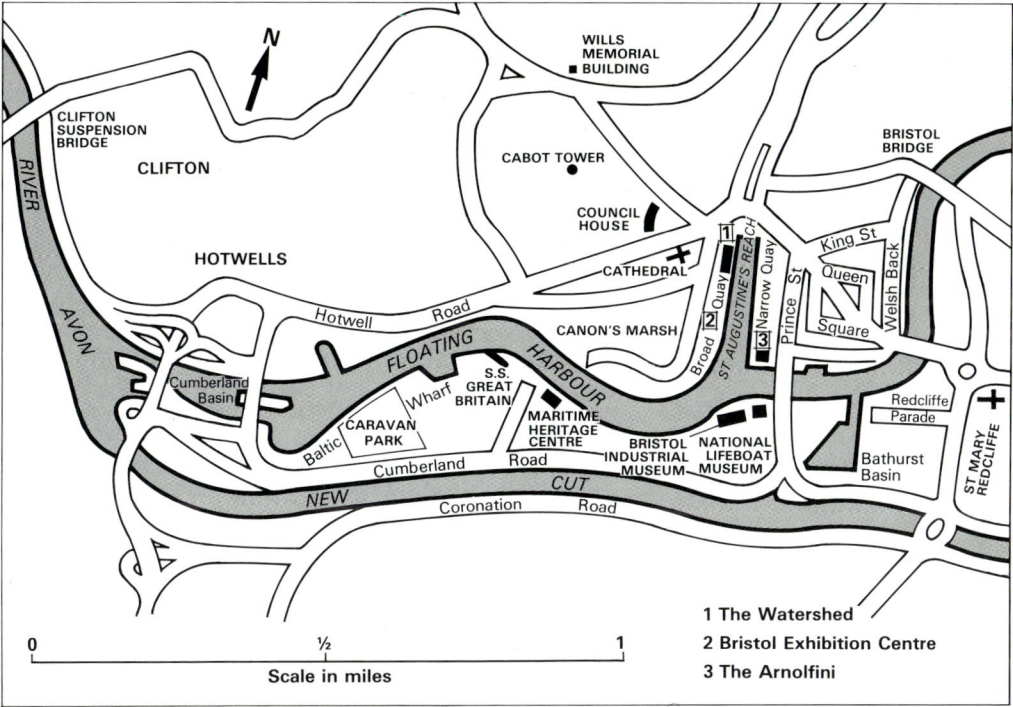

21

best views in the city – across the harbour to the cathedral with the university tower behind. To the left is Cabot Tower, built in 1897 to commemorate the 400th anniversary of John Cabot's voyage to North America.

On Wapping Wharf, further along, are the new Maritime Heritage Centre and the SS *Great Britain,* displayed in the very dock from which she was launched in 1843 by Prince Albert.

A rewarding circular walk, starting from the statue of Neptune, takes you across Queen Square and over Redcliffe Bridge. This offers a good view along Welsh Back to Bristol Bridge and the heart of the old city. You cross by St Mary Redcliffe, so this magnificent church can conveniently be visited at this time. Almost opposite the west end of the church, Redcliffe Parade

runs high alongside the harbour, offering some splendid views across Bristol. Before the road turns at the end, go down to the right, noting the red stone which gave the area its name. You come out at Bathurst Basin, beside the picturesque Ostrich Inn. With its pleasure boats, inns, restored waterfront cottages and warehouses, and new houses, this has become an oasis in the centre of the city. Cross the bridge to Merchants Landing, and then detour along Princes Wharf (by the Industrial Museum). The way back is simple: cross Prince Street Bridge and walk left round the Arnolfini and back along Narrow Quay.

The western end of the floating harbour, at Cumberland Basin, offers the best views of the suspension bridge and the Clifton terraces stretching along their hillside. To the south side is the Nova

Scotia pub, opposite a pretty terrace of dock cottages; beyond are Baltic Wharf with more new housing, and Albion Dockyard with its marinas and boat-repairing businesses. There is pedestrian access to the water-front throughout this stretch, and a public walkway is planned for the whole of the floating harbour.

To the north is Hotwells, which achieved a brief period of fame as a fashionable spa. The water at Hotwells may no longer be prized for its medicinal qualities, and the harbour may no longer generate trade for the city; yet the city docks now offer an unmatched combination of healthy activity and commercial opportunity – a combination of which modern Bristol is proud.

Bathurst Basin – a good example of revival in the heart of the city

Entertainment

King Street may be the 'museum street' of Bristol, but this should not be thought to imply solemnity. Here is Bristol at its most boisterous, with the sounds of jazz from the Old Duke, beery Bristolian laughter from the Naval Volunteer, and heavy rock music from the Granary round the corner.

Here too is the Theatre Royal, the oldest working theatre in the country, and home of the Bristol Old Vic Company. The grand entrance is, in fact, the eighteenth-century façade of the Coopers' Hall, but inside the restored theatre of 1766 has a rare glitter and intimacy. Many famous actors and actresses have performed here, and their signed photographs can be seen in some King Street pubs and restaurants.

The oldest of Bristol's pubs is probably the Hatchet in Frogmore Street, now overshadowed by a very much newer entertainment centre. The timber-framed pub gained its licence in 1606, but it had been a farm outside the city before this. The best story of any Bristol inn comes from the Hole in the Wall, named after its small spy-holes built to watch for predatory press-gangs. Did Robert Louis Stevenson have this pub in mind when he wrote of the 'Spyglass' where Jack Hawkins met Long John Silver in *Treasure Island?*

Jazz and beer may seem best suited to the atmosphere of Bristol's salty seaport, but these are not the only forms of entertainment available. The Hippo-

Below: *The Theatre Royal – the oldest working theatre in England*

Top right: *The Arnolfini – innovative arts centre in an old tea warehouse*

Bottom right: *New housing and new hobbies at Baltic Wharf*

THE HATCHET

ALL H

FROGMORE ST

FOOD
available
MONDAY TO SATURDAY
12:00–2:00 5:30–7:00

FUNCTION ROOM
for Hire

ENJOY A MEAL
IN BRISTOLS
OLDEST PUB

TAVERN
FAYRE

drome offers a variety of shows from popular entertainment to opera; the Colston Hall is the venue for pop and classical concerts.

During the summer the city takes on more of a festival atmosphere, with flags and flowers on the Centre, and special events such as the World Wine Fair, powerboat racing in the docks, and the Balloon Fiesta at Ashton Court.

Far left: *The Hatchet, Frogmore Street, perhaps Bristol's oldest pub*

Left: *The Ostrich Inn has a pretty waterside location at Bathurst Basin*

Below: *The Llandoger Trow – timber-frame and tall gables at their most spectacular*

Clifton is Bristol's Georgian suburb, the place where the town meets the open space of the Downs, and the site of Brunel's suspension bridge across the Avon Gorge. Residents are proud of the atmosphere of 'Clifton Village'; visitors will notice even more – not only does the area have charm, it also offers the unusual grandeur of its setting.

There had been a settlement of farms on the hill above Bristol for several centuries before the area suddenly became fashionable. The popularity of the spa at Hotwells and the desire of the new rich to move out of the smoke and filth of the city encouraged rapid development here towards the end of the eighteenth century. Speculative building began on a grand scale, and despite delays and bankruptcies, the now familiar terraces and crescents were completed. As ever in Bristol, Georgian Clifton lacks something of the politeness of Bath, tumbling as it does higgledy-piggledy down its hillside, but once again, the visitor will find much to explore, and plenty to please and surprise.

A visit should start at the Observatory, beside the suspension bridge. Here, an old snuff mill was converted into an observatory, with a camera obscura giving a secret glimpse of the scene around the tower,

and from here steps lead down to Giant's Cave, which peers out onto the sheer face of the gorge. This is the site of a hillfort, and the views onto the suspension bridge and the gorge are excellent.

Follow the balconied Georgian houses of Sion Hill down beside the bridge, whose 700 ft span is well seen from here. The zigzag path winds down to Hotwells below, and traces of the old funicular railway may still be seen close to the Avon Gorge Hotel. At the end of Sion Hill, climb the steps to Royal York Crescent. (Those with energy should consider a detour down to Windsor Terrace, magnificently sited above the river, and the Polygon, the steepest and most secretive corner of Clifton.) Notice on the right the Paragon, a tightly enclosed crescent whose houses look out on magnificent views, and below, the extent of Cornwallis Crescent. Ahead, you are looking at the longest crescent in England, which now presents a cheerful seaside appearance with its several pastel shades of paint. Follow the raised pavement, with its sweeping views across the docks to the south.

Top right: *Looking along Royal York Crescent - paved walkway, balconies and seaside shades of paint*

Bottom right: *The Mall - Clifton at its grandest*

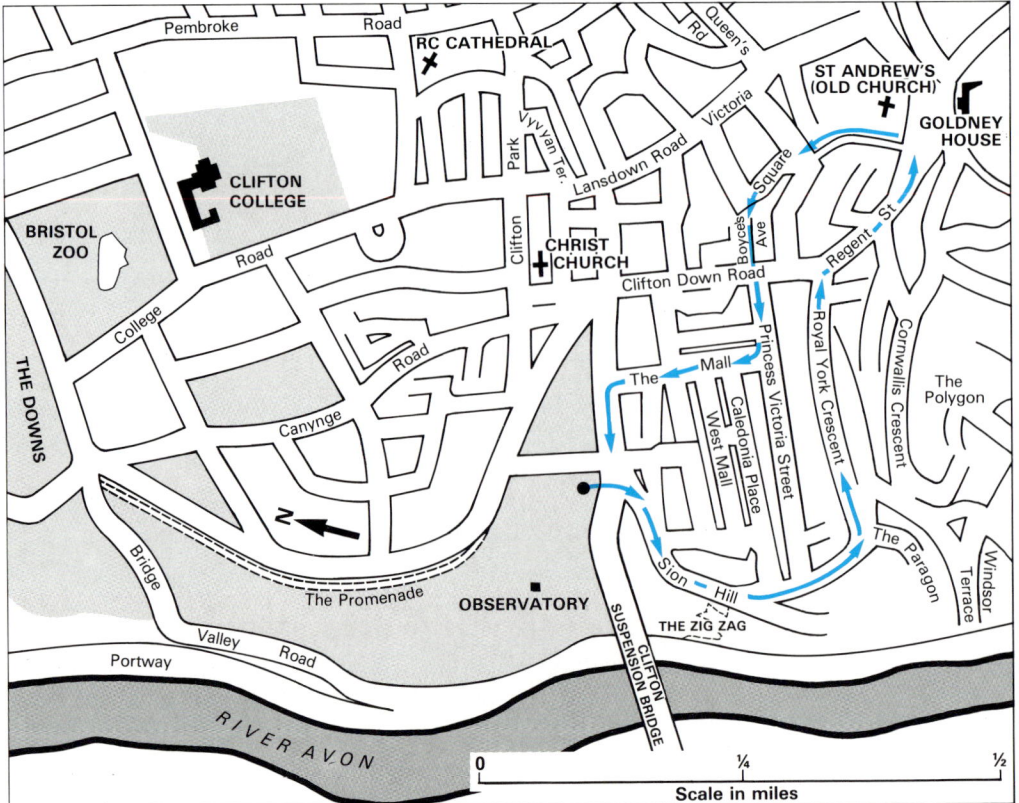

Blue arrows show proposed walk

At the end, turn right to approach the grand houses of Clifton Hill. Among these, Goldney, now part of Bristol University, has an eighteenth-century garden complete with Gothic tower and grotto. Walk through the churchyard of the now-demolished St Andrew's, parish church of Clifton until it became a casualty of the Blitz. Cross Victoria Square, where late Georgian meets early Victorian architecture, and pass through the arch into Boyces Avenue. Princess Victoria Street and the Mall are Clifton's shopping streets, and they lead back to the Observatory and the suspension bridge.

The Clifton Suspension Bridge is a great attraction for visitors, and walking out over the nearly 300 ft gorge to watch the 'toy' cars move along the Portway is exciting. However, the bridge has also proved an attraction to those in despair. In 1885, after a lovers' tiff, Sarah Ann Henley threw herself from the bridge, only to be saved by the parachute effect of her voluminous skirts. She lived to be old.

Victorian Clifton developed to the north, and its most famous sights are the modern Roman Catholic Cathedral, Clifton College, and Bristol Zoo.

Left: *The arch from Boyce's Avenue to Victoria Square*
Below: *Bristol Zoo is a haven of tranquillity within the city*

As Bristol has grown, country villages have been incorporated within the city boundaries, often retaining their distinctive character.

Westbury-on-Trym is at least as old as Bristol itself, and its college is the medieval remnant of a religious house. When William Canynges, the Bristol merchant, turned to the religious life in 1469, he became Dean of Westbury College. Present-day Westbury has some prettily painted stone cottages down beside the Trym, and an impressive parish church.

Henbury is dominated by the Blaise House Estate. Visible from the house is 'Blaise Castle', a Gothic folly on the hill, commanding views of Coombe Dingle (Bristol's other gorge). This whole area of parkland, woodland and craggy gorge is open to the public. But most famous of all Henbury's attractions is Blaise Hamlet, built by the owners of Blaise House for their retired servants; here, ten cottages straggle round a green with a waterpump in picturesquely rural romantic fashion. Each cottage is built of traditional materials – stone and thatch – and each is different. Another unusual Henbury monument, which should be understood as the enlightened gesture it was intended to be, is the headstone and footstone to Scipio Africanus, a negro servant who died in 1720. Black cherubs provide decoration, and the verse records:

I who was born a pagan and a slave
Now sweetly sleep a Christian in my grave.

This grave can be found before the entrance to the church, on the right.

Just outside the official city boundary to the north, but surrounded by suburban development, is Frenchay. This is a surprising village; round the common is a group of imposing eighteenth-century houses; down the hill towards the river, cottages nestle in much less stately fashion. It is possible to walk beside the River Frome through the Oldbury Court Estate to Snuff Mills Park, in another of those places where the countryside invades the city of Bristol.

Right: *Westbury College, a medieval building in an old village*

Below: *A rural dream of stone and thatch at Blaise Hamlet, Henbury*

The City Museum and Art Gallery on Queen's Road contains among its many attractions the natural history collection, displays explaining the archaeology of the Bristol region, and a collection of paintings and sculpture. Elsewhere, other branches of the museum are devoted to a variety of purposes – there's the Industrial Museum, and the St Nicholas Museum with its display on Bristol's history, its collection of church treasures, and brass-rubbing centre. The Red Lodge is an Elizabethan house with exceptional interiors, and the Georgian House gives a glimpse of the life of a wealthy merchant family in the eighteenth century. Blaise House Museum contains a folk collection.

Among Bristol's most popular paid attractions is a visit to the zoo or the SS *Great Britain*. For the best aerial view of the city, climb the Cabot Tower on Brandon Hill, also one of the best places to enjoy a restful few moments in the heart of the city. For more fresh air and exercise, the Ashton Court Estate across the suspension bridge belongs to the City of Bristol, and offers miles of parkland close to the city. Alternatively, head for the Downs, that other great open space, to enjoy the view of the Avon Gorge from Sea Walls.

Top right: *Blaise Castle is a Gothic folly in a magnificent setting*
Centre right: *Inside the Bristol Industrial Museum*
Below: *Perfect Elizabethan interior at the Red Lodge*